SEASONS IN THE SON

a spiritual anthology of poems

In memory of my parents,
Watkin Jones (1899–1974)
and
Mary Lettice Lind Jones (1912–1974)

Contents

Preface

The poems contained in this booklet embrace the Christian Church's liturgical seasons, spanning the period from Advent and Christmas, through Lent, Easter and Whitsun, to Summer, Harvestide, Autumn and All Souls. In so doing, they embrace the close relationship between time and eternity. The theme of the eternal in everyday life, and its impact upon the human spirit is at the heart of each poem.

Three of the poems: *Whitsuntide, Hildegard of Bingen,* and the *Adorable Presence* are included in *A Book of Hours And Other Catholic Devotions* compiled by S. A. Finnegan (Canterbury Press,1998.). Others have appeared in various poetry collections.

The title of this collection of poems came to mind as I recalled a favourite song of mine, which reached the number one spot in the U.K. singles charts in 1974, the year in which I lost my parents. The song was 'Seasons in the Sun', sung by Terry Jacks. The words of one line: "you gave me love and helped me find the sun", comforted me greatly at the time. I was, later, ordained into Christian ministry – and, indeed, into seasons in the Son.

Adventide

In darkness shines the Advent flame,
In light Christ comes, in light he came,
Christ will appear in light the same.

In a sad world so torn and tense
Advent offers the soul a sense
Of joyful hope and penitence.

Christian hearts yearn to tell
Of Christ who conquered death and hell,
The Risen Lord, Emmanuel.

Between the rise and set of sun
The Advent message is but one:
O come, Lord Jesus, come.

Christmas Rush

Buses and bicycles,
Taxis and other vehicles
Weave their way along
A city street past a throng
Of Christmas shoppers in the fading light
With heavy presents, colourful and bright,
A stream of people all of one mind:
To make for home, the place to unwind.

Such activity fails to arouse
The peace and stillness of God's house.
The restless fervour of street and kerb
Cannot God's peace destroy or disturb.
While the expectancy in the hearts of passers-by
Is a seasonal reminder that Christmas will never die,
For humanity is found in a baby's helpless cry
Hallowed in a manger beneath a clear star-lit sky.

Winter Dawn

The peering light of dawn
Disturbs not sleeping Ted
Who lives alone,
The street his home,
A pavement for his bed.

A cold church bright with light
Welcomes the dawning day,
Warm words of love
For God above
Both priest and people say.

There in the morning mist,
At the said Eucharist
Six souls are one
With God's own Son
And in his light exist.

The rousing light of day
Awakes poor, sleeping Ted.
Too weak to stand,
With cap in hand,
He hungers to be fed.

The peering light of dawn
Disturbs not sleeping Ted,
Who now is one
With God's own Son,
With angels round his head.

Christmas Day Service

A solemn procession winds its way
Past the symbolic manger of hay.

In fullness of faith the catholic rite
Points to the Gospel and the crib's true light.

The bishop chants the Eucharistic prayer
While a baby cries aloud here and there.

The Christian faithful bend the knee
To Christ before whom devils flee.

Brother and sister, husband and wife
Before the altar receive new life.

With the Holy Family, all are one
As they praise and adore the new-born Son.

The Holy Nativity

The Christ child from the realm above,
Whom the favoured maiden bore
With meekness and such tender love,
Is Jesus whom we adore.

Sancta Maria, blessed maid,
Your Son was born today,
The Son of God in a manger laid
On a borrowed bed of hay.

The Eastern Sages travelled far
Their richest gifts to bring;
Watched over by their guiding star
They worshipped the heavenly King.

O Holy Babe, the Son of God,
The Saviour of mankind,
Help us to worship you as Lord
With heart and soul and mind.

Light of Love

The bed, the crib,
The bed, the grave,
Our path do pave
Afresh to see
Christ's calvary.
For the light of love,
Our closest breath
Beyond our death
Is Christ above,
A light to lead us
Beyond the tomb
Of death and night
To life and day,
To heaven, a room.

Love's Encounter

O to love our God's compassion
Purging our spirit year by year,
O to love his calm assurance
Melting away each anxious fear.

When the night is dark and lonely,
When our faith and hope grow dim,
His glorious light shines around us,
Shedding true joy that conquers sin.

God's true love, always so constant,
Brings peace and joy to every race,
Our longing ever present
Yearns to meet him face to face.

With his love reaching out to heal us,
With peace and joy ever near to stay,
The eye of faith lights all before us.
Now dawns anew the eternal day.

The Bells of Oxford

From the spire of Saint Mary
To the guardian of the watery snake,
Resounding round the well at Binsey,
Beyond sacred Frideswide ever-awake.

From the stonewashed face of Pusey
To noble Keble's neo-gothic shrine
Beyond All Souls and sacred Aldate
Filling the air with melody divine.

From the bookshelves of Duke Humfrey
To the Tudor splendour of Tom Quad,
Around Greyfriars and Fairacres
In peals of glory to the Triune God.

Gloria, gloria, gloria,
In excelsis Deo.

New Year's Day

Oxford church bells joyfully ring
The old year out, the new year in.
Soon there appears a new ray of light,
Beaming through the curtain of day and night.

Long ago in the dead of night,
The Wise Men honoured the world's true light,
The light who shines in the human heart,
Bidding black sin and darkness depart,
Jesus, whom Christians with one accord
Worship as saviour, master and lord.

Oxford churches this day celebrate
A festival, without pomp and state –
The naming of Jesus, above every other,
And the solemnity of his blessed mother.

The Joyful Mysteries

Mary receives her "highly-favoured" hail
From the lips of the angel, Gabriel.

Mary tells Elizabeth what she has heard,
She is to be Mother of the Incarnate Word.

Mary gives birth, as the angel did say,
In a manger on Christmas Day.

Mary in the Temple presents God's holy Word,
Whom Simeon recognises as the Light of the World.

Mary's child, aged twelve, in the Temple ground,
Deep in discussion with the Doctors is found.

The Mysteries of Light

The Son of God
His ministry begins,
The coming of the Kingdom,
Forgiveness of sins.

The Son of Mary
Performs his first sign,
The coming of the kingdom,
Water into wine.

The Son of Mary,
God's Word from above,
The coming of the kingdom,
Good News of God's love.

The Son of God
In glory does shine,
The coming of the kingdom,
Pure Light divine.

The Son of God
In the Upper Room,
The coming of the kingdom,
Life beyond the tomb.

A Conversion at Sea

Under black, cloudy, foreboding skies,
As Gregory passed from Pharos to Greece,
A dreadful wintry storm did arise,
Which roared and raged and would not cease.

Waves like mountains foamed around,
Threatening to sweep every soul overboard.
Gregory for twenty days and nights was found
In prayer and entreaty to the Lord.

At last he entrusted his whole life
To God who rules o'er land and sea,
At once a steady calm replaced the strife,
At once his holy promises set him free.

(Adapted from *On Himself* by Saint Gregory of Nazianzus.)

Monkswell

The monks of Monkswell kneel and pray
For grace to live in the Christian way.

Early they retire, early they rise,
With heaven to desire and the world to despise.

In prayer and fasting their time is spent,
With virtues to acquire and sins to repent.

With devils to combat and passions to subdue,
Their love is ever steadfast, their love ever new.

God they seek to glorify, their souls to save
Before they face judgment beyond the grave.

A Cloistered Cell

A heavy door lets in a ray
Of early-morning sunshine.
A closed window happily reflects
The gentle new-born light.
On the window-sill a Bible lies open,
The warm pages of Saint John, Chapter One,
Waiting to enlighten the world outside.
The cloistered cell is bathed
In the brightness of God's smile.

The cell, almost empty
Is soon filled with wonder and light,
The golden decor of God's presence.
Its door, the way to life.
Its window, an insight into
Heavenly imaging.
Its Bible, the Logos,
The clear sunshine of God's promises
So often clouded by human problems.

Saint David

From New Menevia
The son of Non and Sant
Brought the message of Christ
To a people in want.

Field and footpath,
Cloister and cell
Cried out with the same:
"Do the little things well."

He lived the Gospel
By Word and Deed
Giving food and shelter
To those in need.

As monk and bishop
Under God's own hand,
He bestowed God's blessing
Upon Dewisland.

Centuries later
He brought Wales fresh hope,
When declared a Saint
By Callistus, Pope.

Pilgrims journeying
Far from home
Aimed for Jerusalem,
St David's and Rome.

For blessed David
And his Cathedra,
For the Incarnate Son –
Deo Gloria.

Henfynyw

The eternal peace of God is found
In Old Menevia's hallowed ground.
Here the dead in Christ find a waiting bed,
Here David and Gustilianus once did tread
Whose prayers now comfort Henfynyw's dead.

Mortal substance returns to the soil,
The end of its struggle, the end of its toil.
Earth to earth returns,
(God alone knows best),
And on its return finds true rest.

Henfynyw's dead will one day rise
To face judgment before God's eyes,
Love will enter Life
Which love has won,
And return to its source, God's only Son.

St David's Cathedral, Pembrokeshire

On a crisp December morn,
The time of year when Christ was born,
Five pious souls kneel
In steady, silent prayer
In the Cathedral chapel
Of the Holy Trinity.

An ageing priest in vestments newly-worn
Approaches a well-worn altar of stone
Where five crosses lie carved
As ageless symbols of endless grace,
A cross for each kneeling soul
Knit to Christ who died for all.

In this hallowed place there is harmony.
Here souls are bonded together in blessed unity,
And moulded into the likeness of
Father, Son and Spirit
By the transforming love of the Holy Trinity.

The Sorrowful Mysteries

In the Garden
The Holy One
In agony prayed,
God's only Son.

At the Pillar
The Holy One
Was stripped and scourged,
God's only Son.

Crowned with thorns
The Holy One
Was mocked and scorned,
God's only Son.

Carrying his cross
The Holy One
Stumbled and fell,
God's only Son.

Nailed to the cross
God's only Son
Died for our sins,
The Sinless One.

The Cross of Christ

Lord, lead us to the rugged Cross
On the hill of Calvary
Whereon you suffered shame and loss
That souls might ransomed be.

Lord, draw us to yourself who came
To die upon that Tree,
Embracing all who love your name
With grace to set them free.

Lord, grant us in each hour of life
Vigour and zeal anew
To preach to all of the new life
That never fades, that is in you.

Resurrection Morning

To church the faithful make their way
For solemn Mass on Easter Day.
In deepest sin and shame they kneel
To await Christ's heart their hearts to heal.
Christ's flock assemble in Christ's name
The Gospel message to proclaim.

The altar bell thrice thrice does ring
To hail aloud the heavenly king
Who as the Risen Christ does give
Himself that ransomed souls might live.
Christ to each, in each does bring
The purest love, love free from sin.

In love they approach the altar throne
As weary pilgrims coming home.
Their sins forgiven, their hearts they raise
In adoration, prayer and praise.
As one in Christ whom they receive,
As one, the altar-rail they leave.

Prayer after Holy Communion

Jesu, gentle saviour,
O saviour, hear our call,
Be with us to inspire
Our hearts with love for all.

Jesu, gentle saviour,
O saviour, our true light,
Be in health our happiness,
Our joy, our great delight.

Jesu, gentle saviour,
O saviour, our true wealth,
In sorrow be our sunshine,
In sickness our true health.

Jesu, gentle saviour,
O saviour in the strife,
In danger be our comfort,
In death our promised life.

Eastertide

The twilight gloom of six long weeks,
Which veils the narrow way
Is scattered by a radiant light,
The light of Easter Day.

The paschal candle burning bright,
In darkness sheds a beam,
For Christ, our Saviour, came and died
Our nature to redeem.

One Church above, one Church below
In love and joy prevail,
And alleluias now are sung
The Risen Christ to hail.

And when our Eastertide is spent
And Easter anthems o'er
Jesus still meets us in our need
With plenteous love in store.

(Modelled on *Candlemas*, by Cardinal John Henry Newman.)

The Blessed Sacrament

Before the Blessed Sacrament
We slowly bow the knee
In honour of our Saviour
Whom faith alone can see.

Before the Blessed Sacrament,
· Our sinful deeds we tell,
In wonder at his Presence
Where lasting peace does dwell.

Before the Blessed Sacrament
Our longing hearts we raise
In solemn adoration,
With might and reverent praise.

Before the Blessed Sacrament
We bless the Three in One,
In Unity proceeding,
Till all our days are done.

Whitsuntide

Holy Spirit from above,
Sweet Comforter most dear,
Inspire us with your love,
To restless souls draw near.

Holy Spirit from above,
Your sevenfold gifts impart,
Inspire us with your love,
Seek out the pure in heart.

Holy Spirit from above,
Tongue of eternal fire,
Inspire us with your love,
Become our souls' desire.

Holy Spirit from above,
Grant us to know your peace,
Life-giving Holy Dove,
Bid all our striving cease.

The Holy Trinity

Blessed be God,
Who gave his Son to save
His unworthy children
With life beyond the grave.

Blessed be Jesus,
Who gave himself to feed
God's weary children
With strength in time of need.

Blessed be the Spirit,
Who is given in love
By Father and by Son
To comfort from above.

Eternal Moment

O Eternal Moment,
Heaven sent
The Spirit to outpour
On an earthly tent,
Sweet fellowship divine,
The Pentecost of time.

O Eternal Moment,
Heaven sent,
Where mercy and grace
Are found in embrace,
Opening Paradise,
Absolving sins and lies.

O Eternal Moment,
Heaven sent,
Soul-glowing breath,
Comfort in death,
Repose of the sleeping,
And hearth of the living.

O Eternal Moment,
Heaven sent,
Forever the same,
Love by name,
Flowing and free,
Life's melody.

Holy Hour

It is holy hour
When Word and Sacrament
Shining bright
Cast a ray of heavenly light.

It is holy hour
When the Christian faithful
Here and there
Kneel in contemplative prayer.

It is holy hour
When fourteen stations call
All to see
The cost of love on Calvary.

It is holy hour
When sorrow and hurt are
Lost in peace
And souls experience love's release.

Strata Florida

A weathered arch welcomes the weary traveller
To the rugged ruins of a Cistercian House.
It stands at the boundary of time and eternity,
Where time has stood still for over seven centuries.
It is an entrance to a forgotten world,
A window into heaven.

In the stillness of Strata Florida,
Where the healing hands of Christ reach out
To a restless, broken world,
The ordinary is infused with the sacred,
Ancient stones are transformed
Into tablets of holy living,
Earth and heaven are held together by prayer,
And valley, hill and sky are one.

Amid its ruins the Spirit breathes life
That cannot change, that is always new,
Wherein love and joy, peace and rest are found,
Rest for the travelling Giraldus and Baldwin,
And eternal rest for Dafydd ap Gwilym.
Such is the unfading glory of Ystrad Fflur.

Abbey Station, Saint Honorat

At Abbey Station I begin my journey.
There are no pumps, no petrol,
No revving engines, no changing gears,
Only cloister, altar, choir,
The music of nature and the chanting of *frères*.

Here the fuel of travel is grace,
Flowing unseen,
Eternal and endless.
Grace to love,
Grace to work,
Grace to pray
For those alive and those who have died,
Spirit-given, Spirit-supplied,
Gift from God, God as gift.

Travelling, I reflect upon gift and giver,
The created and creator,
The purpose and passage of time,
And the distance from Sinai to Galilee
Which cannot be measured in miles or kilometres
But in terms of offer and rejection,
Sin and forgiveness.

Accompanied by faithful prayer
I continue my inward journey,
Towards divine providence and meaning,
Heavenly thought and desire,
Nearness and belonging to the God
Of Bethlehem and Calvary,
The empty tomb and eternity:
My destination and destiny.

Worship at Lérins

Bowing before the silence
Of altar,
Chanting in the silence
Of choir,
Addressing the silence,
Living fire,
In holy Word and prayer.

Embracing the silence
Of holy Virgin and Child,
Hallowing the silence
Of hanging, wooden cross,
Partaking of the silence
Of Word made Flesh,
Gazing upon the silence
Of sacrament exposed.

Listening to the silence,
Breathing the silence,
Loving the silence,
Becoming the silence:
The silence of God.

Sisters of Silence

A knock summons the waiting nun.
She bows in reverence,
And, with head still bowed,
Leads the priest in silence to the sacristy,
Past two rows of sisters
Clad in black and deep in prayer.

She helps the priest to vest.
He recites the prayer of preparation,
Before approaching the altar of God,
To offer bread and wine in sacrifice.
Priest and religious
Are enveloped in prayer.
O, how the sweet stillness of prayer
Enlivens the soul!

All are fed and refreshed
From paten and chalice.
The day arrives.
The priest leaves.
The outer silence is broken.
The inner silence remains.

Hildegard of Bingen

A ray of shining light,
Of pure, creative energy,
Poured through the open window
Of God's grace,
Stirring the spirit of Hildegard
And filling her mind with warmth,
Insight and fullness.

Her spirit awoke,
Her mind expanded,
Her heart, refreshed with the dew
Of her baptism,
Rejoiced in the beauty of creation,
Her soul experienced the wonder
Of Christ's risen life.

She found freedom in faith,
Freedom like the freedom of a feather
Blown about by the breath of God,
While the soft springs of the Spirit
Moistened her wilting heart,
Germinating the divine seed within her,
Making what had withered, green.

A mirror of dazzling light,
A "symphonia" of divine harmony,
A spring of living water,
A source of joy and healing,
A living symbol of a loving heart,
A green branch for all time,
Became this "Sibyl of the Rhine."

Mother Julian of Norwich

Julian, saved from early death,
In faithful prayer would kneel,
Without a word, a cell her world,
God's "shewings" to reveal.

Prayer comforts the inner self
As only love can tell,
"Prayer oneth the soul to God,"
Wrote Julian in her cell.

Love alone can purify
The wounds of sin and shame,
God looks upon his loved ones
"With pity, not with blame."

Faith and hope can overcome
Deep sorrow and despair,
Led on by the light of love
And quiet, steadfast prayer.

Believing "all shall be well"
Comforts the troubled breast,
Knowing God's "meaning is love"
Brings peace and joy and rest.

God's sixteen "shewings" of love,
By word and story told,
Still echo around the world
From Julian's anchorhold.

Glorious Mysteries

Jesus is raised on Easter Day,
Opening for us the heavenly way.

Jesus ascends high above
Into the glory of his Father's love.

The Holy Spirit, heavenly flame,
Descends at Pentecost in Jesu's name.

Blessed Mary at death's sigh
Is taken up to heaven on high.

She who showed a Mother's love
Is crowned Queen of heaven above.

The Virgin Mary Of The Fourvière

The morning mist hangs heavily
Over the *quais* of the Saône
Like a portrait of the nether world.
From the haze a young woman emerges,
Her slender arms and shoulders
Pushing along her well-wrapped babe
As she endeavours to balance
A freshly-baked breadstick
Between her tender fingers.

Gradually, the mist lifts
And the late-May sun breaks through
To reveal the hill-top above the "old quarter",
Where I behold the Virgin Mary of the Fourvière
Looking over, looking after the Lyonnais
With maternal care; she whose *"fiat"*
To the Angel's message long ago
Gave birth to the Son of God,
"The Bread of Life".

In the silence of the evening hour,
Surrounded by candles and icons,
A priest celebrates the Sacred Mysteries,
And I recall the day's mystical experiences in rhyme:
From darkness to light,
The breaking of bread,
The freshness of morn,
The need to be fed.
The Child in the manger,
God becoming Man,
God's eternal childhood,
The baby in the pram.

Birth and motherhood,
Redemption and Fall,
Mother of Christ,
Mother of all.
The rising of sun,
The close of day,
The mystery of life,
God, a breath away.

A Weary Pilgrim

A weary pilgrim sits in the nave of a church,
His spirit uplifted by the image of the
Christ-child in the arms of his Mother.
He is soon enveloped in stillness,
The stillness which is Christ's gift to the world,
The stillness of love, the stillness of God.

The old covenant has been fulfilled.
God has come in Christ at the willingness
Of a young virgin to bear the Lord of life,
The Messiah, the heavenly manna
In a spiritual wilderness,
The holy grandchild of Joachim and Anna.

The weary pilgrim is touched
By God's presence, peace and power –
Not the destructive power of the world
Where violence reigns,
But the strengthening power of gentleness
And the healing power of humble love.

The Adorable Presence

With peeping pace and silent step
They pass the sleepy nest of books
Imprisoned under lock and key
Beneath the ever-watchful gaze
Of two-faced time.

Soon touched with holy awe they cross
Themselves and see with wakened eyes
Christ himself gazing lovingly,
Surrounded by his Mother blest
And the heavenly company.

They yearn to utter the splendour
Of heaven's everlasting joy,
They yearn to quench their thirsty souls
Upon the tears of Christ divine.
Such yearning is also mine.

An Open Heart

A briefcase-carrying soul
Is drawn by a beacon of light
In the south porch,
And the welcome of an open door.
He crosses a busy street
During the rush hour,
· To offer thanks and praise
To God, his heavenly Father.

He kneels at the evening hour
Before the Mother and Child most fair.
His briefcase rests against
A straw basket cradling
Decades of votive candles.
Candles and hanging lamps
Burn everywhere
With the fire of living prayer.

It is six. The Angelus is rung.
A service advertised as *Mass*
Begins in the chapel beside him.
He is lost in prayer at the *prie-Dieu,*
Lost in an oasis of silence,
Where a deep-flowing stream
Of living water has formed
A spring within his heart.

Another miracle,
Another act of grace,
As deep answers deep,
And heart speaks to heart,
As a new channel flows
To water an open heart,
To refresh a thirsty soul
For whom Christ is all in all.

He leaves.
The Eucharist continues
According to the Anglican rite.
He belongs to the See of Peter.
All is catholic in the widest sense.
An open heart
Disappears beyond
An open door.

Notre-Dame du Port

By a harbour in Nice
Where grand yachts lie afloat,
Stands a church to Our Lady,
Notre-Dame of the Port.

As Queen of the Angels
She guards night and day
The paths of wayfarers
Crossing the Bay,
Who, before a voyage,
Pray with all their might
To the blessed Trinity
And the saints in light.

The church is ablaze
As votive candles burn
In thanksgiving
For a safe return:
Father, Son and Spirit,
God of land and sea,
For your love pour moi,
Merci. Merci.
Notre-Dame du Port,
Star of the sea,
For your prayers pour moi,
Merci. Merci.
Sainte Thérèse of Lisieux,
Saint Jean Vianney,
For your prayers pour moi,
Merci. Merci.

In the chapel of Saint Joseph
Stands Saint Peter in his boat,
Holding the Keys and Bible,
Midst the sanctuary of the port,
While the palms outside,
Bowing and waving, bring
Unspoken hosannas
Before the heavenly king.

Midsummer

June is fresh
And June is sweet,
Its sun throws
Sufficient heat.

Flowers bloom
And green leaves dance
To create
A summer trance.

June performs
A one act play
In praise of
The longest day.

Scenes are set
In cloudless blue,
Birds sing out
Clear and true.

Lovers yearn
To breathe its air,
Lovers find
Its days most fair.

June is gone
Winter is near,
June once more
Will soon be here.

Summer Glory

The bare branches of winter
Bow towards the barren soil,
Mourning their loss in silence,
Leafless and lifeless,
Unable to hide their sorrow,
Unable to cover their shame.

Their creator, seeing their sorrow,
Covers their nakedness
With an alb of fine snow,
A symbol of purity,
Before renewing his promise
Of new life and new birth.

The divine promise is fulfilled.
The leafy branches, finding shelter
From the burning sun,
Rejoice in their rich clothing
While the Father embraces the Son
In a blaze of summer glory.

Arundel

A white-robed procession of swans
Graces the smooth-flowing Arun,
Surrounded by the season's green frontal.
They stoop and quench their thirst,
They cross, and feed their hunger
Upon floating crusts along Arun's bank,
In a liturgy of nature.

A prevailing rock nearby stands,
Steeped in houses and history,
With a castle and cathedral.
The one an emblem of resistance,
The other a symbol of tolerance;
Fellow-witnesses to the ebb and flow
Of worship upon an ever-shifting shore.

The procession encircles the sanctuary,
While love and gentleness,
Joy and hopefulness,
A heavenly oneness,
Sing in harmony
Softening the air
Around Arundel.

Saint Seraphim of Sarov

He dwelt in inner peace
Amid a wilderness of trees,
His home a bare hermitage
Far from the cry of humanity,
His life a communion with the saints,
As one with life's pattern
Of creation and redemption,
Through constant intercessory prayer.

In the great forest of Temniki
His vision of glory became a space
For Christ to enter.
His silence found a dwelling
In many searching hearts.
Divine light radiated
From the heart of this "saint of silence",
Whose joy was the risen Christ.

Harvest Festival

Fruits and flowers and vegetables all
Are brought to the church for harvest festival.
A large congregation turns up for the feast
And awaits the arrival of preacher and priest,
Who, with panting breath, hurry along
To begin the Harvest Evensong.
Relatives and friends are lost in delight
As they hear their little ones sing and recite.
Some stand at the back, or in the aisles made narrow
By extra chairs, turnip and marrow.
The guest preacher climbs the pulpit stair,
With cough and whisper here and there.
His long sermon over, he returns to his seat
To the shuffle of restless bodies and feet.

The church hall now becomes the venue,
With rows of tables, and high-tea, the menu
Bread and butter, cheese and jam,
Sandwiches of egg and ham,
Meringues, trifles and cakes of every kind
To help those present relax and unwind,
Are consumed at a steady rate,
With the passing of plate after plate,
Until plates and tablecloths are clear
And high-tea is over for another year.

Clergy and people soon are gone
But memories of their time live on.
Their Evensong continues in the realm above,
A thanksgiving for a harvest of God's love.

Autumn Leaves

Autumn leaves find no pleasure in the sun,
They fall on the pavement one by one.

Autumn leaves, crinkled and old,
Provide a carpet of yellow and gold.

Autumn leaves know their end is near
At the setting of another year.

Autumn leaves are withered and gone
Before they can hear the angels' song.

Hymn to the Angels

Holy angels from above,
Holy messengers of love,
Keep us vigilant, we pray,
When the tempter comes our way.

Holy angels from above,
· Holy messengers of love,
Defend the Church here below
From Satan, the sleepless foe.

Holy angels from above,
Holy messengers of love,
Keep us on the narrow way
Lest we stumble, fall or stray.

Holy angels from above,
Holy messengers of love,
Protect us from our earliest breath
To the hour of our death.

Christian Service

Every Christian prays to be
In the love of God immersed,
With the love of God inspired,
By the love of God upheld,
And alive in Christ for all to see.

Every Christian lives to take
The love of God to others,
See the love of God in all,
Serve the Son, the servant king,
With the fruits the Spirit does bring.

Eulogy To Saint John Roberts

In early manhood
You entered Christ's priesthood,
The way of the Cross.

You kept the faith of old
And suffered for Christ's fold,
The way of the Cross.

You faced Calvary
On Tyburn's tree,
The tree of the Cross.

We remember you with praise,
Today and all our days,
Saint John Roberts of Wales.

Solemn Worship on All Souls

Priests in vestments black as
Good Friday afternoon
Approach the high altar
Of a college chapel,
With its dark cross, the tree of life,
For solemn worship on All Souls.

Plainsong echoing from high walls
And fan-vaulted ceiling,
From lengthy nave and wide sanctuary,
Becomes a plainsong from the past,
Echoing down the ages,
During solemn worship on All Souls.

Candles, bells and incense,
Elevations and genuflections,
Greet the Risen Christ,
The living word, the word made flesh,
The sacrament of eternal life,
During solemn worship on All Souls.

An echo is heard in the empty chapel,
An echo from beyond the Cross
And empty tomb, the gate of glory,
An echo of gentle assurance and approval
From the Lord of the dead and the living,
After solemn worship on All Souls.

"For everything there is a season,
and a time for every matter under heaven."
Ecclesiastes: chapter three, verse one.
(Revised Standard Version)

Notes

These poems are a reminder of the continuity of the Christian faith, like a river, over the centuries – be it through prayer and contemplation, or silence, solitude and self-abandonment, or celebration and thanksgiving. They span the First and Second Millennia to the present day.

The First Millennium

Saint David, Patron Saint of Wales, was educated at the small Celtic monastery of Henfynyw (Old Menevia), near Aberaeron, West Wales, in the sixth century by Gustilianus, a gifted teacher of his day. The missionary zeal and activity of David and his fellow monks was such that they managed to keep the Christian faith alive among the Britons in the face of heresy and paganism. Their endeavours also helped to preserve the Welsh language, which has been spoken since post-Roman times.

   The Church at this time and throughout the Millennium was undivided. Sea trade and traffic from the Mediterranean to Ireland and much of Britain would pass along West Wales. As a consequence, Celtic monasticism came under the influence of the monasticism of the Eastern Mediterranean, and the teaching of the Fathers of the Early Church. *A Conversion At Sea* is about Saint Gregory of Nazianzus (c329-c390), one of the Cappadocian Fathers.

The Second Millennium

Schism between Christian East and West occurred in 1054.

Saint David's Cathedral (the site of Saint David's monastery) was completed in 1181 under Peter de Leia, a Norman bishop. Saint David was eventually canonised during the pontificate of Callistus II (1119-1124.) At the same time, Pope Callistus decreed that two pilgrimages to Saint David's equalled one to Rome, and that three equalled one to Jerusalem.

At **Strata Florida**, West Wales, can be seen the ruins of a once-thriving Cistercian abbey. It is historically important for being the burial place of Welsh princes and of Dafydd ap Gwilym (1340-1370), the greatest Welsh poet of the Middle Ages. Baldwin, Archbishop of Canterbury, visited the abbey in 1188, during a visit to Wales to preach the Crusades. He was accompanied on his travels by Giraldus Cambrensis, or Gerald of Wales, (1146-1220), the great scholar-priest and traveller of his day.

The influence of holy women in the Middle Ages is significant. **Hildegard of Bingen** (1098-1179) was a Rhineland mystic and abbess of a Benedictine monastery near Mainz, Germany. She was a playwright, composer and poet as well as a naturalist and visionary.

Mother Julian of Norwich (1342-1418) was an English mystic and anchoress, who for many years lived and ministered in a cell attached to Saint Julian's church, Norwich. Her book, "The Revelations of Divine Love", has become a spiritual classic.

Saint John Roberts (1577-1610), from North Wales, is another Welshman canonised during the Second Millennium. He was martyred at Tyburn, London.

Saint Seraphim of Sarov (1759-1833) was a Russian Orthodox monk-priest, who spent twenty years in solitude, in practice of prayer. He became spiritual guide to many throughout Russia.

The Third Millennium

Many of today's devotions, such as the rosary, have their origins in the Middle Ages.

See: *The Joyful Mysteries, The Sorrowful Mysteries, The Glorious Mysteries.*

See also: *The Blessed Sacrament, Holy Hour, Solemn Worship on All Souls.*

Particular reference is made to the motherhood of the Virgin Mary, who was declared "Mother of God" by The Council Of Ephesus in 431.

See: *The Virgin Mary of The Fourvière, A Weary Pilgrim, The Adorable Presence, An Open Heart, Notre-Dame du Port.*

Witness to the Christian faith through a life of silence and solitude is celebrated in the following:

Monkswell, A Cloistered Cell, Eternal Moment, Worship at Lérins, Sisters of Silence.

Poems where the sacred and secular come together are also included:

Christmas Rush, Winter Dawn, The Bells of Oxford, Midsummer, Summer Glory, Arundel, Harvest Festival, Autumn Leaves.

Additional Notes

The Bells of Oxford

L1 Saint Mary: Saint Mary, the Virgin, the University Church.

L2 the guardian of the watery snake: Magdalen College.

L3 The well at Binsey: the well dedicated to Saint Margaret, outside Binsey Church.

L4 Frideswide: The Patron Saint of Oxford.

L5 the stone washed face of Pusey: Pusey House.

L6 noble Keble's neo-gothic shrine: the chapel of Keble College.

L7 All Souls: All Souls' College.

L8 sacred Aldate: Saint Aldate's Church.

L9 Duke Humfrey: the oldest part of the Bodleian Library.

L10 Tom Quad: the south, east and west sides of the Great Quadrangle at Christ Church.

L11 Greyfrairs : the Franciscan church in Oxford.

L11 Fairacres : the Convent of the Sisters of The love of God at Fairacres.

Abbey Station, Saint Honorat
Saint Honorat: a tiny island which together with Sainte Marguerite makes up the Isles of Lérins situated in the Bay of Cannes. Saint Honorat founded a monastery there in 404. Today, the island is home to a thriving Cistercian community.

Worship at Lérins
A reference to worship at the Cistercian abbey on Saint Honorat.

The Virgin Mary of The Fourvière
The hill of the Fourvière (Lat. *Forum Vetus*) is the site of a settlement in Roman times. Its large basilica and statue of the Virgin overlook the city of Lyons.

Solemn Worship on All Souls
All Souls' Day falls on November 2nd.

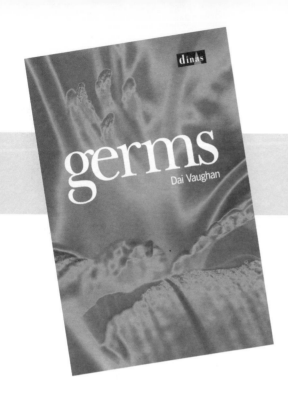

Germs

Dai Vaughan

Short stories: a fiction in 77 unrelated episodes for the intelligent general reader.

"Examines how minds work and what fiction is in a most original way."
— **Caroline Clark, www.gwales.com**

£5.95

ISBN: 0 86243 708 3

Cunval's Mission

David Hancocks

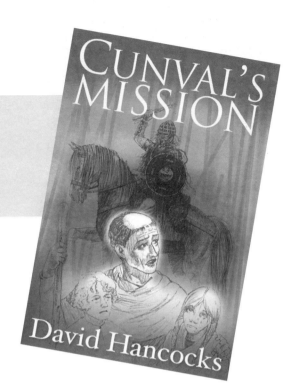

Cunval, a newly-ordained priest is given a territory to convert to Christianity, leading to may exciting incidents.

"Read on! This reviewer couldn't put the book down!"
– **James Coutts, www.churchinwales.org**

£5.95

ISBN: 0 86243 709 1

Titles already published

For more information about this innovative imprint, contact Lefi Gruffudd at lefi@ylolfa.com or go to www.ylolfa.com/dinas. A Dinas catalogue is also available.